Thoughts of The Gifted On Entrepreneurship Volume 1

Compiled By
Joseph S. Moshood
Gladstar Gifted and Talented School

https://www.gladstar.sch.ng

FOREWORD

As a man thinks so is he. We need to learn from those that are dynamic practitoners of entrepreneurship by reviewing and meditating on their thoughts. We are presenting snapshots on entrepreneurship that can make you stand out,get ahead in business , make money, save money, avoid worry, cash in on bargains, gain social advancement, avoid embarrassment, avoid boredom, gain prestige and attain security in old age.

pamaconsultingsarl
@pamaconsulting1

.

May 18
Every thing is possible if you put your mind to it and you really work hard and bring the right perpective to it #millionairemindset **#Entrepreneurship** #PositiveVibes

Business kits
@businesskits007

.

May 19
Don't ever think everyone is going to buy from you, even Coca-Cola that survived two world wars have people that have never tasted any of their products. You always need to have a target market. **#Entrepreneurship** #SmallBiz #startup

Facilitating Functional Education For The Next Innovators, Entrepreneurs and Leaders.

nethmin95
@nethmin95

May 13
"What should Our Business Be ?" by Nethmin

link.medium.com/n1RhSyEBs6 . . #entrepreneur #business #motivation **#entrepreneurship** #success #entrepreneurlife #smallbusiness #marketing #inspiration #love #money #startup #businessowner #hustle #goals #lifestyle #mindset #realestate

The Rebel Entrepreneur Series
@TheRebelSeries

May 18
Rebel entrepreneurs do business on their terms and with freedom in mind
#Entrepreneur **#entrepreneurs** #blog #blogger #Careers #freedom #success #business #businessowner #startup #innovation #Entrepreneurship

Don't do it for money. Do it for freedom - FULL ARTICLE

Rebel entrepreneurs are able to take that plunge and do it for freedom. They work when they want, where and how they want. They don't do it for money.

therebelentrepreneurseries.com

Entrepreneur ME
@EntMagazineME

6m

With the #COVID19 crisis, we don't know when we will go back to normal, or even what the new normal will look like, but what we do know is that this will pass--so, as #entrepreneurs, what you should do now is to make sure you're prepared for the future:

Facilitating Functional Education For The Next Innovators, Entrepreneurs and Leaders.

Getting Through The COVID-19 Crisis: Tips From One Young Entrepreneur To Another
These unprecedented times are creating trials for many, but however testing they may seem, with those challenges, come opportunities.
entrepreneur.com

@GoI_MeitY

Entrepreneur Quotes
@KmibsCom

.

May 19
"What good is an idea if it remains an idea? Try. Experiment. Iterate. Fail. Try again. Change the world." - Simon Sinek #entrepreneurs

Payout
@Payout06997853

.

May 19
The 5 Biggest Mistakes Entrepreneurs Make

Expecting success right away.

Trying to do everything yourself. ...

Facilitating Functional Education For The Next Innovators, Entrepreneurs and Leaders.

Ignoring your true passion and just going for the money.

Not being adaptable. ...

Ignoring social media. **#entrepreneurs** #Businesses #failure

What should Our Business Be ?
Identifying proper business objectives
link.medium.com

Chris Goettel
@chrisgoettel

.

May 13
Your "weakness" is your opportunity. **#entrepreneurship** #vulnerability

Your "weakness" is your opportunity. — Chris Goettel
For entrepreneurs, the problem that haunts you may just set you free.
chrisgoettel.com

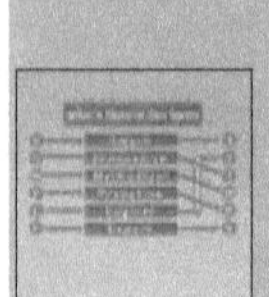

SUHAS AGAWANE
@SuhasAgawane

.

May 13

Facilitating Functional Education For The Next Innovators, Entrepreneurs and Leaders.

Hope U r liking this week's #MySimpleQuote There is scarcely any passion without struggle. Here we hv our embedded advert on this week's theme 'Struggle' #entrepreneurship #startup #innovation #creative #Passion #infosecurity #dataprivacy #datasecurity #Simple #Slimpe

ZIWO
@ZiwobyAswat

.

May 13

Why is API Key to your business? Read More _ziwo.io/why-is-api-key_..... #API #integration #crm #apisecurity #developers #software #technology #gulfstartup #smeuae **#entrepreneurship** #innovation #ideas #coding #fullstack #frontend #backend #javascript #softdev #devops #fintech #KSA

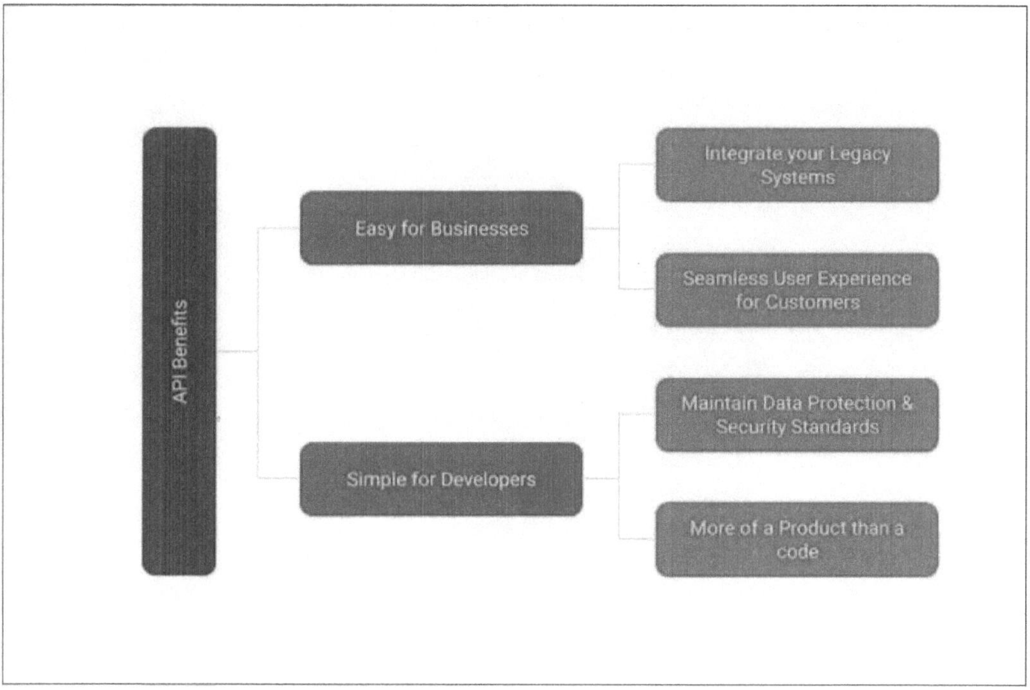

Why is API key to your business? | Contact Center Software | ziwo.io

Facilitating Functional Education For The Next Innovators, Entrepreneurs and Leaders.

This blog explains the basics of API management and the benefits of API which is key to your business.
ziwo.io

Thom Ruhe
@ThomRuhe

.

May 13

The power of #ecosysteming **and #entrepreneurship**! Durham AND Raleigh are Ranked: The 10 US Cities Best Positioned To Recover From Coronavirus via
.forbes.com/sites/laurabeg_________...
@ncidea
@AmerUnderground
@HQRaleigh
@FirstFlightOps
@RloTonSocial
@startupsUSAorg
@KauffmanFDN
@CEDNC

Ranked: The 10 US Cities Best Positioned To Recover From Coronavirus (And The 10 Worst)
Coronavirus recovery: What it will look like across America.
forbes.com

John Hall
@johnhall

May 13

'The true entrepreneur is a doer, not a dreamer." - Nolan Bushnell #Entrepreneurship

Facilitating Functional Education For The Next Innovators, Entrepreneurs and Leaders.

Worklings
@worklings

May 13

Customers are a very important part of any business and creating value for them is just as essential. Check out today's video which focuses on Customer Relationships. #worklings **#Entrepreneurship** #CustomerExperience #StayHomeStaySafe

Shashira HP
@ShashiraHP

22m

Always SEE it from the CUSTOMER'S point of view #marketing #customers #CustomerExperience #customersupport #advertising #contentmarketing #marketingstrategy #marketingtips #marketingstrategy **#Entrepreneurship** #Entrepreneurs #entrepreneurlife #business

Flexibility in your business model helps you cope with unforeseen circumstances and sudden changes in the market. #Entrepreneurship

derek rundell
@derekrundell

.

May 15

Entrepreneurs, who run startups that withstand the test of time, constantly ask questions. Be open to change. Be adaptable. Ask for feedback. Test your limits. #startups #entrepreneurship #success #founders #teamwork

Creating the Foundation for a Timeless Startup | StarterNoise
We often think of startups as high-paced, but not all need to move at the speed of light. Here's how to create the foundation for a timeless startup.
starternoise.com

ExcelCapitalGroup
@ExcelCapitalGr1

.

23h

Business Credit Myth: Companies automatically have a business profile with the credit bureaus. Business owners actually have to apply for a DUNs number with Dun & Bradstreet, the major business credit reporter, before their profile is compiled. #businesscredit #Entrepreneurship

Build
Business
Credit
BEFORE you
need it.

@EXCELCAPITALGROUP

DNT Digital Services
@DigitalDnt

14h
Motivation can only get you so far in the journey of **#Entrepreneurship** . Discipline is what grows your #Business

The whole idea of motivation is a trap. Forget motivation, just do it.

John C. Maxwell

DNT Digital

Saud Juman
@SaudJuman

May 21

I hit an ideation block exploring new health tech ideas. Mentors taught me to create the Mastermind effect with at least 1 other person that compliments my skillset to launch something impactful. Struggling w/o the tech half of my mastermind brain. #ideation **#Entrepreneurship**

Shaktia
@joinshaktia

8m

Wisdom comes from many places. Today, we're working on our fears that stops us from moving forward in life. What messages will you receive that you need to pay attention to? **#Entrepreneurship** #onlinemoney #holistichealth

Naval Gupta
@naval_gupta

.

11m

Be aware of your environment. What do you think about it? **#Entrepreneurship**
#Entreprenuer

You become what you surround yourself with. Energies are contagious. Choose carefully. Your environment will become you.

Rahil Sipai
@RahilSipai

May 14
Learn from your failures, take time to organize your thoughts after a failure and identify where you went wrong. #Entrepreneurship

PamH
@PamH86769510

1m

It is time for everyone to be equipped to create their own job, have entrepreneurial practice. Education has let us down, many are not prepared for the new economy. My team and I have scalable solutions for **#Entrepreneurship** and accelerating #success

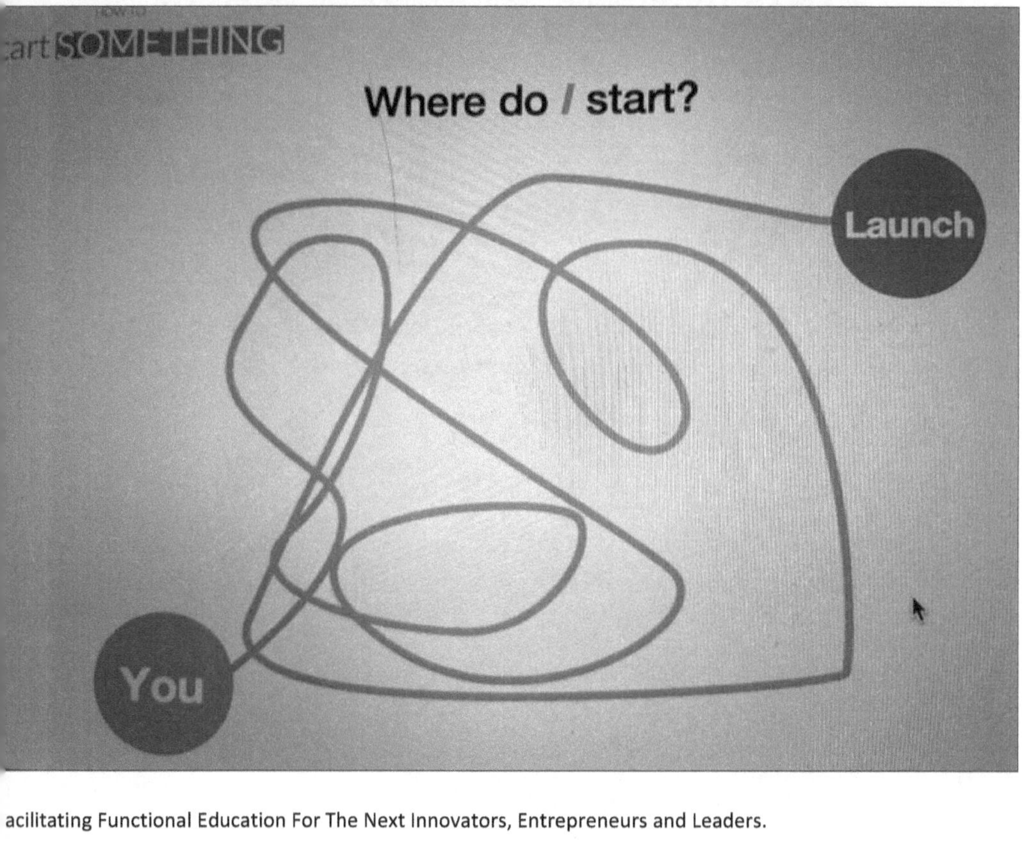

Facilitating Functional Education For The Next Innovators, Entrepreneurs and Leaders.

IPCH International
@ipchintl

May 18

It's no longer a competitive edge to be in one category or another. To bring most value, one must be an innovative disruptor. #entrepreneurmindset **#entrepreneurship** #startups

Forbes

"Successful people today are both innovators and disruptors — they create something that was not there before."

DHANIN CHEARAVANONT
Senior Chairman of CP Group

13

Bilal Jafar
@bilaljafar00

May 14

Get yourself out of the comfort zone **#Entrepreneurship** #startup

Evan Kirstel #MasksForAll #RemoteWork
@evankirstel

May 15

Smart small, dream big #FridayThoughts #founders #startips **#Entrepreneurship** #entrepreneurs

Ron & Sandy Lee
@SandyLeeAndRonS

19h

Try to work at least some part of each day on those small things!

#entrepreneurship #opportunities

Facilitating Functional Education For The Next Innovators, Entrepreneurs and Leaders.

Andy VanDyke
@AndyvDyke

May 19

The best way to predict your future is to create it! **#Entrepreneurship**

The best way to predict
the future is to create it.
AndyVanDyke.com

Laura
@yeoengland

.

May 19

Research. Test. Review. The basics of tweaking your way to success. **#Entrepreneurship** #Covid_19

Money_Making_Motivator
@MegaMinds11

.

May 22

Startups Killers.Just beware of these. #BusinessMan #BusinessNews #Motivation #startups #MiLLiONS **#entrepreneurs** #Entrepreneurship

MISTAKES THAT KILL STARTUPS

SINGLE FOUNDER

MARGINAL NICHE

DERIVATIVE IDEA

OBSTINACY

HIRING BAD PROGRAMMERS

CHOOSING WRONG PLATFORMS

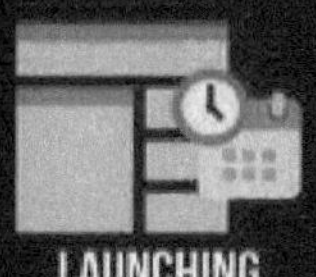

SLOWNESS IN LAUNCHING

LAUNCHING TOO EARLY

NOT WANTING TO GET YOUR HANDS DIRTY

publicspeaking_coach
@Maz06170846

Throwback to my #keynote at the **#entrepreneurs** summit. Businesses aren't built in a day. You have to stay self driven, hungry be okay to fail and have an unshakeable faith in what you're building. I'm blessed to... instagram.com/p/CAIhQHMB5pg/...

Patrick Carney
@Carney_ART

May 21
#CovAIDFestival "Build a community around your product. They will buy the product and will stay for the community." - Ryan Deiss #ScottDuffy **#Entrepreneurs**

Dermisho Enterprises
@dermisho_ent

Facilitating Functional Education For The Next Innovators, Entrepreneurs and Leaders.

May 23

Success is beyond what you know... #Dosomething **#entrepreneurs** #dermisho

Our strength is not in what we know, but in what we do.

#Fact check
#Dermisho Enterprises

Facilitating Functional Education For The Next Innovators, Entrepreneurs and Leaders.

BASIC BUSINESS CYCLE
RESEARCH
YOUR
BUSINESS
REVIEW
TEST
YOUNG
ENTREPRENEURS
OF ENGLAND

h

To be successful, you have to be patient in all the times, because opportunity knocks without any notice and only the patient lot will grasp it. #Business #Entrepreneurship
sabcnews

Facilitating Functional Education For The Next Innovators, Entrepreneurs and Leaders.

Lennart
thebusinessgoat
APPLE IN 1976
APPLE IN 2020
GOOGLE IN 1998
GOOGLE IN 2020
AMAZON IN 1994
AMAZON IN 2020

Lifted Finance Consulting Ltd
@FinanceLifted

10h
#Entrepreneurship is not an easy road. You became an entrepreneur for a reason; you had a great idea & you have a passion for pursuing this idea to make a difference. For me, my biggest success has often followed from trying #JUSTONEMORETIME after hitting the brick wall of defeat

Reminder
Flexibility is an essential component of your business plan
Options
Close
DEADLINE
12
3
9
6